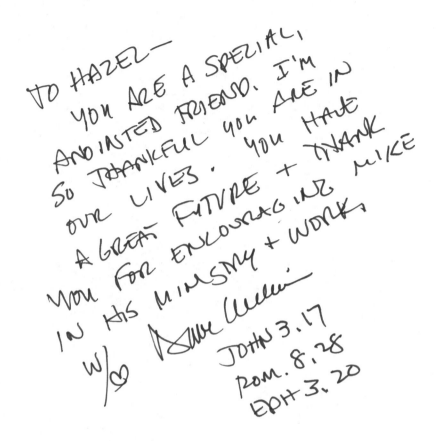

TO HAZEL —
YOU ARE A SPECIAL,
ANOINTED FRIEND. I'M
SO THANKFUL YOU ARE IN
OUR LIVES. YOU HAVE
A GREAT FUTURE + THANK
YOU FOR ENCOURAGING MIKE
IN HIS MINISTRY + WORK,

W/♥ Dave Williams

JOHN 3.17
ROM. 8.28
EPH 3.20

YOUR SPECTACULAR MIND

BY

DAVE WILLIAMS

YOUR SPECTACULAR MIND
UNLEASH YOUR GOD-GIVEN POTENTIAL

978-0-938020-72-1

Cover design by Timothy Henley
Illustrations by Mike Tomanica

DECAPOLIS
PUBLISHING

Printed in the United States of America

OTHER BOOKS BY DAVE WILLIAMS

ABC's of Success and Happiness
Angels: They Are Watching You
Beatitudes: Success 101
The Beauty of Holiness
Coming Into the Wealthy Place
The Desires of Your Heart
Developing the Spirit of a Conqueror
Elite Prayer Warriors
Emerging Leaders
Faith Goals
Filled
Genuine Prosperity
Gifts That Shape Your Life and Change Your World
Have You Heard From the Lord Lately?
How to Be a High Performance Believer
How to Help Your Pastor Succeed
The Imposter
Jezebel Spirit
Miracle Breakthrough Power of the First Fruit
Miracle Results of Fasting
The New Life…The Start of Something Wonderful
The Pastor's Pay
Pacesetting Leadership
The Presence of God
Private Garden
Radical Fasting
Radical Forgiveness
Radical Healing
Regaining Your Spiritual Momentum
The Road to Radical Riches
Seven Sign Posts on the Road to Spiritual Maturity
Skill for Battle
The Spirit of Antagonism
Toxic Committees and Venomous Boards
What to Do if You Miss the Rapture
The World Beyond
Your Pastor: A Key to Your Personal Wealth

For more information regarding Dave Williams'
pacesetting ministry products please go to
www.davewilliams.com

CONTENTS

FIRST THOUGHTS 9

YOUR MIND: DESIGNED FOR SUCCESS 15

MIND RENOVATION 19

MIND TOXINS 25

UNSOUND FRIENDS 31

THE DEVIL MADE ME DO IT 35

THE POWER OF RIGHT THINKING 39

STEPS TO SUCCESS 49

THE LOST ART OF MEDITATION 61

WHAT YOU GAIN 69

HOW TO MEDITATE IN A BIBLICAL WAY. 77

YOUR TERRIFIC MEMORY 83

THE LAST WORD 101

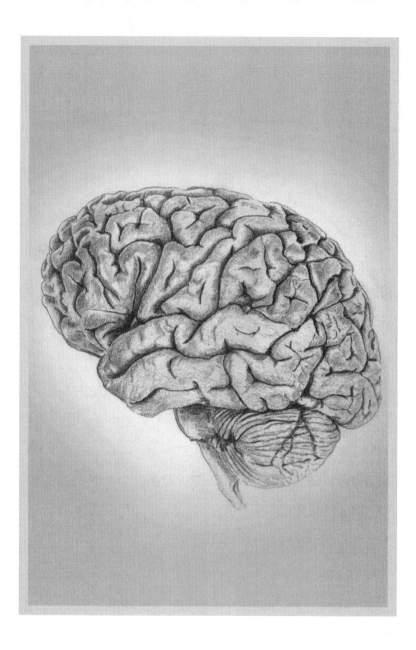

The human brain—a miracle of God's creation.
What does God's Word reveal about the mind's abilities?

FIRST THOUGHTS

The mind is one of the most amazing gifts God has given to mankind. A mind is a special, unique, ultra-powerful tool that God has infused with enormous capabilities.

Many people think the mind and the brain are one and the same, but that is not true. The brain is a purely physical entity. [1] [2] [3]

- If you are an adult, your brain weighs about three pounds. Compare this to an elephant's brain that weighs twelve pounds or a squirrel's brain that weighs one quarter of an ounce.

- The adult human brain is about two percent of total body weight.

- Almost 80 percent of your brain is comprised of water.

- The total surface area of your brain is 2.5 square feet.

[1] *Brain Facts and Figures,* University of Washington website: http://faculty.washington.edu/chudler/facts.html#brain.

[2] Blinkov, S.M. and Glezer, I.I., *The Human Brain in Figures and Tables: A Quantitative Handbook*, Plenum Press, New York, NY, 1968.

[3] Nieuwenhuys, R; ten Donkelaar, H.J. and Nicholson, C., *The Central Nervous System of Vertebrates*, Vol. 3, Springer, Berlin, Germany, 1998.

An untrained mind is a waste of potential power—like a rocket
parked on the launching pad going nowhere.

- Your brain has about 100 billion neurons. Compare this to an octopus brain that has about 300 million neurons.
- If the blood supply to your brain is cut off, you will lose consciousness in nine seconds.

But the mind is much more than these statistics about the brain.

Scientists have only begun to understand the brain, and they are a long way from understanding the mind. However, we have another important source that reveals volumes about the mind:

- How to care for the mind
- How to use the mind
- How to renew the mind

That source of knowledge regarding the mind is the Holy Bible. The Bible tells us that our minds are:

- A gift from God
- A magnificent tool
- A vital link to our success

Yet many minds are flabby, lazy, and untrained. Some Christians never develop their mind "muscle," so it remains like a NASA rocket parked on the launching pad—so much potential that is unused and going nowhere.

This book will show you how to take that rocket ship, tune it up, and launch it into orbit. This book will show you how to develop your mind as a powerful tool that will help you excel in every area of life and ministry.

Have you ever wished you could train your mind for success rather than failure? This book will show you how.

Have you wished your mind were sharp like a razor rather than dull like a butter knife? This book will help you renew your mind and regain its powerful abilities.

Have you ever wished you had a better memory? This book will show you ways to improve your ability to remember things.

Have you wished you could make God's Word part of your daily thoughts? This book will help you train your mind to focus on the things that are important to God.

By focusing on a few basic principles and useful practices, this book will give you keys to using and caring for your spectacular mind. You will find yourself:

- Remembering more
- Feeling more relaxed
- Having greater mental clarity
- Cultivating healthy thoughts
- Growing closer to God

Let's not waste another minute. Read on to discover the marvelous abilities God has given us in our spectacular minds.

Dave Williams
Lansing, Michigan

Why do some succeed and some fail?
Somehow the mind's spectacular possibilities
get mired down and wasted.

CHAPTER 1

YOUR MIND: DESIGNED FOR SUCCESS

Have you noticed that some people sabotage their lives? Ruin their marriages? Drive their businesses into the ground? Have you known someone who was moving ahead in life but one day, for no apparent reason, he or she bailed out? Have you seen people destroy their lives by purposefully damaging important relationships?

I have seen people do things like this almost unconsciously and then wonder what happened. They blame the devil or other people but never look at themselves.

I have always wondered why some people succeed and prosper while others attain a certain degree of success and then do something to sabotage it. Were they destined to fail? I don't believe so. The problem was in their minds. Somehow the mind's spectacular possibilities were mired down and wasted.

Does this mean that smart, well-educated people succeed, and not-so-smart, under-educated people fail? No. I used to think that the smarter and better educated you were the more success you would enjoy, but I found out there were men and women with PhDs standing in line at the unemployment office.

I also read about men like Lee Braxton. Lee only had a sixth grade education, but he always wanted to be a bank president. A tragic event had forced him to quit school and work to support his family. When he was old enough, he went to the bank and applied for a job. The personnel director said, "You don't have even a high school diploma—we can't use you."

So, Lee started his own bank, which eventually grew to be the largest bank in the state. Then he bought more than a dozen other businesses that also succeeded. The city's people loved him because he was a kind, benevolent man who gave generously to many charities. They elected him mayor of the city. Lee had no education to speak of, but his mind carried him further than most people even dream possible. He was considered to be a brilliant man.

Then there is the story of Harland Sanders. He was not an educated man, but he had a recipe and a dream. He tried to sell his recipe to restaurants and was rejected time after time. So, one day he built his own restaurant and named it Kentucky Fried Chicken. People loved his chicken so much they said, "Harland, this idea is too big for just one restaurant. You ought to franchise it." Though he was already in his sixties, he started franchising his chicken recipe and the rest is culinary history.

INTENTIONAL SUCCESS

Both these men did something right, something meaningful, and something wonderful for themselves and others. I believe the source of their success began in the way their minds worked. There is no such thing as accidental success. Success is always intentional, and every success starts in the mind.

I am sure that no one begins a venture intending to fail. No one opens a business, goes to college, gets married, or has children thinking that one day the venture or relationship will come to ruin. No one plans for his or her own destruction. Self-sabotage is unconscious. It happens, and we don't know when it started or why. It creeps up on us like a heart attack. The failure comes suddenly, but actually it is the result of years of neglect and bad choices.

What are the main ingredients of self-sabotage? There are two:

- Wrong thinking
- Faithless, negative friends

People like Lee Braxton and Harland Sanders—and a dozen others you could name from your own observation—listened to the right people and fed their minds the right input. How do we follow their example? In the following chapters, we are going to discover what your mind really is, how to care for it, and how to tap greater levels of your mind's potential.

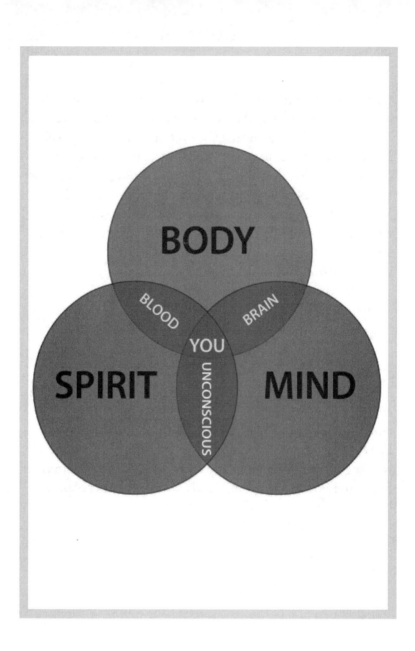

God created us as a spirit, a mind (also called the soul) and a body, so that we are a little "reflection" of the Holy Trinity—the Godhead.

CHAPTER

MIND RENOVATION

Where is the mind? Does it have a location in our body? Is it an organ like the liver or the heart? Is it a part of our brain or spinal cord? Can it be cut out and examined by scientists? The answer is no. The mind is not a physical organ; in a sense, it has an eternal nature. It goes on after our physical body has died, just as the human spirit lives on. You can kill the brain, but you can never kill the mind.

The Bible calls the mind the "soul." The Greek word for it is *psyche*, from which we get the words psychology and psychiatry. God created us as a spirit, a mind (also called the soul), and a body, so that we are a little "reflection" of the Holy Trinity—the Godhead. In the universal sense, these three aspects of man are so interconnected that it is often difficult to tell what is of the mind, of the spirit, or of the body. In fact, these three elements often overlap.

For instance, physical illness can make you moody or depressed. Likewise, a tragic emotional event can cause actual physical illness. On the other hand, a touch from God in our spirit can heal our bodies and fill us with joy. How the three

When Adam sinned, he literally lost his mind—or at least its capacity
to work perfectly—and so did the rest of us.

elements of man—spirit, mind, and body—operate together is a great mystery. In fact, the writer of the book of Hebrews said that only the Word of God could divide that which is soul (mind) and that which is spirit.

> For the word of God is quick, and powerful, and sharper than any two edged sword, piercing even to the dividing asunder of soul and spirit, and of the joints and marrow, and is a discerner of the thoughts and intents of the heart.
>
> —Hebrews 4:12

We can see it this way: the mind is like the manager of a large corporation, and the brain is like a huge mainframe computer that the mind has at its disposal. When the mind receives direction from our spirit—the part of us that God speaks to—it goes into action, directing the brain, body, and emotions to act accordingly. The mind filters out bad information and passes on good information. It polices our feelings and tells us how to act, what to read, what to watch and listen to, and where to go.

The brain is the servant of the mind. The mind is the servant of the spirit. The spirit is the servant of God. At least, that's how God intended it to be. As you will see, it doesn't always work that way.

THE FIRST MIND

When God breathed life into Adam, he gave him a mind and brain that worked at one hundred percent capacity. Can you imagine that? Scientific research reveals that humans use less than five percent of the brain's capacity. Five percent! Adam was off the charts in his brilliance and intelligence. He was literally a super-genius. If the average American has an

I.Q. of 115, Adam's was twenty times that; his I.Q. was over 2,000! How else was he able to name and catalog all the plants and animals God created? There are millions and millions of different creatures crawling and vegetation growing on the earth, and Adam classified and remembered them all. Only a fully functioning brain could take on that monumental task.

When Adam sinned, he literally lost his mind—or at least its capacity to work perfectly—and so did the rest of us. We don't know if it happened suddenly or if, over the ages, the brainpower humanity originally possessed declined gradually. It appears to have leveled off now. In either case, we do know that the mind became corrupted and dragged down by sin. It is one of mankind's greatest tragedies.

But there is good news! Jesus came to our fallen world to create a whole new species of being, reclaiming the territory that was lost in the fall of man. That includes regaining the human mind's capacities. Until a person is born again, he retains the old nature of humanity that can never use more than a fraction of his brain's potential. Why? Because his mind is clouded, weighed down, and corrupted by sin. However, once man is born again his nature is changed, and he begins to regain the mind's capacity that was lost in the fall. Once saved, he can develop the mind of Christ, little by little, precept upon precept, line upon line.

> [9] **Whom shall he teach knowledge? and whom shall he make to understand doctrine? them that are weaned from the milk, and drawn from the breasts.**
>
> [10] **For precept must be upon precept, precept upon precept; line upon line, line upon line; here a little, and there a little....**
>
> **—Isaiah 28:9–10**

Our goal as Christians is to possess the mind of Christ. God breathes that desire into our spirit when we are born again. But our spirit is hindered by our poorly cared for and corrupt mind with its reduced capacity. Your spirit cries out to be fed spiritual food, to be close to God and to obey everything in the Bible, but your mind rebels.

An unrenewed mind is the biggest hindrance to spiritual growth and success in any area of life.

For true mind renovation, you must decide what thoughts are
allowed in and what thoughts stay out. If the input
isn't worthy, close your mind to it!

CHAPTER

MIND TOXINS

Therefore if any man be in Christ, he is a new creature: old things are passed away; behold, all things are become new.

—2 Corinthians 5:17

As believers, we know that our spirit was recreated the moment we accepted Christ as our Savior. The Bible says,

I tell you for certain that everyone who hears my message and has faith in the one who sent me has eternal life and will never be condemned. They have already gone from death to life.

—John 5:24 (CEV)

One of the greatest things about salvation is that you do not have to work for it. God gives you a recreated spirit the moment you accept Christ. Praise God!

But salvation does not immediately change everything about you. For example, when you became saved your body was not instantly recreated. If you were overweight when your spirit got saved, you were still overweight one minute later.

If you were skinny, out of shape, or scrawny—none of that changed. Wouldn't it be nice if it did?

This is also true of your mind. You do not instantly receive a newly programmed mind, a perfected thought process, or a whole new set of memories. In the same way that an overweight person has to exercise and eat right to change his or her physique, you must "exercise" and "eat right" to renew your mind.

> ¹ I beseech you therefore, brethren, by the mercies of God, that ye present your bodies a living sacrifice, holy, acceptable unto God, which is your reasonable service.
>
> ² And be not conformed to this world: but be ye transformed by the renewing of your mind, that ye may prove what is that good, and acceptable, and perfect, will of God.
>
> —Romans 12:1–2
>
> And be constantly renewed in the spirit of your mind [having a fresh mental and spiritual attitude]....
>
> —Ephesians 4:23 (AMP)

FRIENDS AND FOOD

The first step in realizing the potential of your spectacular mind is to examine your friends and your food. What friends do you keep, and what "food" do you put into your mind? These two things determine the kind of mind you are developing. First, let's look at the food.

Where does wrong food originate? You have a wide array of food choices to feed your mind in this sin-scarred world. There is, of course, the Bible, which is an endless cornucopia of nutritious spiritual food. There are thousands of other "food" choices as well—some godly and some not.

26

You have received a large amount of input from your culture. From the time you were born, you were programmed in certain ways. Not all of the programming is bad. For instance, your parents programmed you to say "please" and "thank you," to wash your hands before eating, to obey those in authority over you, and to be polite.

Some cultural values, like fair play and kindness, are found across cultural divides. Other cultural norms are unique to certain places. In the United States, it is customary to greet each other with a handshake using the right hand. In parts of Europe, it is customary to kiss on each cheek as a greeting. In Japan, it is customary to greet one another by bowing. I have heard that in China it is considered a compliment to the cook to belch during and after a meal. In the United States that would be considered quite rude.

There are spiritual customs as well. In some countries, wearing neckties is considered demonic because they point downward. In other countries, to not wear a necktie is a sign of disrespect.

In South Africa, when a preacher steps into the pulpit he is considered very unspiritual if he does not say something like this: "I greet you in the glorious, majestic, holy name of Jesus." Whenever I receive a letter from a South African Christian, the opening phrase is always something like, "Hello, my dear brother. I greet you in the matchless, powerful Name of the Lord Jesus Christ, the Name above all names."

When I first traveled to South Africa I did not know about this custom. So, when I arose to the platform to preach I said, "Hello, and greetings from the United States of America. It is great to be here." The congregation probably wondered why there was an unsaved man in the pulpit?

Since then I have learned to say, "I greet you in the glorious, majestic, wonderful, all-powerful, all-consuming, loving Name of Jesus Christ of Nazareth!" I figure the more adjectives I put in my greeting, the more they will respect what I have to say! Of course, if I used a similar greeting in the United States, people would think it was strange.

Mount Hope Church sent a team of people to Brazil for a short-term mission trip. We did not know that in Brazil a woman is considered to have loose morals if she laughs in public. One of our pastors preached about the revival that had hit our church, and he mentioned the holy laughter experienced by some of the women. He talked about how the joy of the Lord was so strong on them that they would laugh and giggle and laugh some more. All the while, the Brazilian audience must have been wondering why American women had such bad moral principles.

TOXIC FOOD

Most of the time, cultural input is just different; it's not inherently good or bad. However, some cultural input can be very harmful. You have heard the expression, "Garbage in, garbage out." This means you can only get out what you put in. If garbage goes in, then only garbage can come out. Your mind receives a tremendous load of input from your cultural environment. Television, music, magazines, advertising, newspapers, and books constantly shout what you need, what is acceptable behavior and what words and actions are okay to speak and do. Sometimes your spirit can barely stand up in faith after a barrage of negative or ungodly input.

Jesus meant for your spirit to be the number one priority. Then your mind should be subject to your spirit and your body subject to your mind. However, many Christians live like animals. Their body rules their mind and spirit. They feed their spirit for one hour on Sunday, and expect to be spiritually full the rest of the week. All the while, they are programming their minds with unprincipled television programs where any behavior seems to be acceptable. As a result, they are mentally stunted.

If you are to renovate your mind for success and victory, you must take hold and regulate the input. You must decide what goes in and what stays out. Like a faucet—lefty loosy, righty tighty—you must evaluate the worthiness of the input and then open or close your mind to it.

When you have unsound friends they feed you garbage.
Their garbage goes into your mind and
garbage—bad decisions—comes out.

CHAPTER

UNSOUND FRIENDS

Friends can be even more influential than culture in shaping your thoughts and actions. When you have the wrong set of friends, it can sabotage your success and create thought patterns that limit your mind's potential.

There is a terrific example of how this works in 1 Chronicles.

> ¹ Some time after this, King Nahash of the Ammonites died, and his son Hanun became king.
>
> ² David said, "I am going to show loyalty to Hanun because his father, Nahash, was always loyal to me." So David sent messengers to express sympathy to Hanun about his father's death. But when David's ambassadors arrived in the land of Ammon,
>
> ³ the Ammonite commanders said to Hanun, "Do you really think these men are coming here to honor your father? No! David has sent them to spy out the land so they can come in and conquer it!"
>
> 4 So Hanun seized David's ambassadors and shaved them, cut off their robes at the buttocks, and sent them back to David in shame.
>
> —1 Chronicles 19:1–4 (NLT)

Hanun lost his father and was crowned king. David had been friends with Hanun's father, so he sent an envoy of ambassadors to comfort him. It was a magnanimous gesture on the part of King David. But Hanun's defective friends convinced him that David was up to no good. So, instead of receiving David's envoy with honor, Hanun had their beards shaved off and cut their clothes so they were exposed. In other words, he publicly humiliated them.

Needless to say, David did not look kindly on this treatment of his representatives. So, he sent his army and his top commander to settle the score. God was on David's side and the Ammonites were soundly defeated.

> **2 And David took the crown of their king from off his head, and found it to weigh a talent of gold, and there were precious stones in it; and it was set upon David's head: and he brought also exceeding much spoil out of the city.**
>
> **3 And he brought out the people that were in it, and cut them with saws, and with harrows of iron, and with axes. Even so dealt David with all the cities of the children of Ammon. And David and all the people returned to Jerusalem.**
>
> **—1 Chronicles 20:2–3**

David had sent the envoy out of kindness, but Hanun was listening to unsound, spurious friends. Their advice caused Hanun to commit a terrible injustice. Within one year, the cities of Ammon were wiped out and looted, and the people were enslaved. David took Hanun's crown and placed it on his own head. Hanun was destroyed.

That is what happens when you have the wrong friends. Their garbage goes into your mind and garbage—bad decisions—comes out. They cause you to do foolish things. A handful of the wrong friends can do you as much harm as a thousand enemies.

When I first became a pastor in 1981, many of my "friends" in ministry told me there could never be a great church in Lansing because the city had a "Samson spirit" over it. One of the people who told me this seemed to be very spiritual and "holy." He even prophesied several other things about my ministry. Another pastor told me, "There will never be a great church in Lansing because there are too many political demons in this capital city." In the end he and these other friends were proven wrong.

I'm glad I didn't accept their counsel. Jesus said we would cast out demons, not let them run our cities. Not too many years after these so-called friends made these predictions, Mount Hope Church was thriving, and the mayor invited me to be the grand marshal of Lansing's Memorial Day parade. Mary Jo and I rode in a convertible waving to all the people lining the parade route. We were literally at the head of the procession, and when I looked behind us there came the senators, congressmen, councilmen, and all the rest of the so-called "political demons" on foot!

If I had listened to those unsound friends, I never would have sought to influence the city or build a big church. Thank God I had many other friends who encouraged me with sound advice and wisdom.

You can try to blame the devil for all your sins,
but the true culprit is your unrenewed mind.
"The devil made me do it!" is not an acceptable excuse.

CHAPTER **5**

THE DEVIL MADE ME DO IT

Some Christians don't want to give up their off-target friends or their favorite television shows, so they blame their lack of success on the devil rather than the wrong input.

Once a father asked his little girl, "Why did you make your brother cry?" She responded, "The devil made me kick him and pull his hair, but I thought of biting him all by myself." I have a feeling she thought of all three of those misdeeds by herself.

Many of the problems caused by our unrenewed minds get blamed on the devil. A woman once said to me, "Pray for me. The dirty devil is trying to get me to gamble. I'm going out again tonight, so pray the devil won't make me gamble."

"Where are you going tonight?" I asked.

"To the casino!" If she was serious about not gambling, what was she doing going to the casino?

A father told his son, "I don't want you to swim in the gravel pit; it's too dangerous." One day he caught his son at the gravel pit carrying a pair of swimming trunks. "What are you doing here with your swimming trunks?" he asked.

"I just brought them along in case I was tempted to swim," the boy answered.

We blame too much of our bad behavior on the devil. How many times have you heard someone say:

- "The devil destroyed my marriage."
- "The devil wrecked my business."
- "The devil ruined my ministry."

Whenever I hear people say things like that, I want to scream out, "Jesus said, 'I give you power over the enemy.' Quit feeding yourself garbage, get into the Word of God and you won't be blaming the devil for everything!"

> **Behold, I give unto you power to tread on serpents and scorpions, and over all the power of the enemy: and nothing shall by any means hurt you.**
>
> **—Luke 10:19**

You become vulnerable to the devil when you are lax in renewing your mind. It takes mental energy to resist the devil, and a "flabby" mind usually can't stand up to him. What happens if you do not feed your body? It shrivels up. What happens if you don't feed your mind? It will shrivel up, too. You can look at a man who is forty-five or fifty years old and he looks fit. Then you talk to him for a minute and realize he sounds like a third-grader. He has not fed his mind. He is not stupid, and he certainly has the capacity to learn, but he has not used it.

The devil preys on people with weak minds, people who choose the wrong mental diet and associate with defective friends. They are easy pickings for Satan. But if you renovate your mind, you will have the upper hand. God gave you a mind that is powerful enough to resist the devil—with the help of the Holy Spirit. The only way you can fail is if you neglect to renew your mind.

Think of Jesus when he was tempted in the desert (Matthew 4:1–11; Luke 4:1–13). That encounter was largely about Jesus' willingness to obey God. He had the ability to choose otherwise—as do you. The devil tried to get Jesus to obey his stomach by telling him to turn stones into bread. The devil tried to get Jesus to obey his mind by offering him all the kingdoms of the world if Jesus would worship him. But Jesus' spirit, mind, and body stayed in perfect submission to the Father, and the devil couldn't find a way to gain mastery over him.

The devil goes after you in the places where your mind is weakest. You must feed yourself a steady diet of pure, perfect, spirit food to stay strong. Where do you get it? It comes through God's Word. In John 6:63, Jesus said, "The words that I speak to you are spirit and life." And in Romans 10:17, Paul said faith comes by hearing the Word of God. The Word is spiritual food. You need to stop blaming the devil and reprogram your mind to desire other things; that is how to gain victory over your situation. Just like an overweight man reprograms his mind to demand less food, and a recovering drug addict fights the mental urge for drugs, you must reprogram your mind with God's Word if you want to be successful.

No one wants to cross the finish line of the race of life still making excuses about how the devil robbed him or her of victory. I have the feeling God will tell the people who try to excuse their failures, "I gave you the tools to defeat Satan, but you preferred to blame him so you could hold on to ungodly, destructive things in your life."

God's Word reveals his plan for you to become a "right thinker." Read on to discover how you can renew your mind.

What are you telling yourself?
Are you feeding yourself the right input?

CHAPTER

THE POWER OF RIGHT THINKING

Bad input from your culture and friends is damaging, and the devil's attacks can be challenging, but the most damaging input comes from within yourself.

> **All the days of the afflicted are evil: but he that is of a merry heart hath a continual feast.**
>
> **—Proverbs 15:15**

This means that your mind-set determines what kind of life you will have. For the afflicted, every day seems evil, but for the person who chooses to be happy, life is one long, sumptuous buffet table.

You have enormous power to choose your thoughts, your mental posture, and what you believe. Your mind can be your best friend or worst enemy. Let me give you an example of the cycle you can fall into with wrong thinking.

1. WRONG INPUT leads to WRONG
   CONCLUSIONS

2. WRONG CONCLUSIONS lead to WRONG ACTIONS
3. WRONG ACTIONS lead to DEFEAT

On the other hand...

4. RIGHT INPUT leads to RIGHT CONCLUSIONS
5. RIGHT CONCLUSIONS lead to RIGHT ACTIONS
6. RIGHT ACTIONS lead to SUCCESS!

We believe our own words far more than we believe other people's words. What are you telling yourself? Are you feeding yourself the right input?

I read about a forty-six year old man who died leaving behind a loving wife and four beautiful children. From the time he was thirty-eight, all he talked about was how the men in his family died at a young age. His grandfather died young. His own father died young. So, from the time he was thirty-eight years old he began to make preparations so that his family would be taken care of when he died. He got the right insurance policy and drew up a will. When he went to the doctor for an examination he told him, "All the men in my family die young, and probably I will die young too."

Sure enough, at age forty-six, his heart stopped just as he said time and again it would. He wrote the script for his life, and that script led to an early death.

RESETTING THE MIND

On the other hand, I know a man who, for years, used to drink a fifth of whiskey every day. He accepted Jesus as his Savior and determined to renew his mind, to feed it the right thoughts instead of the wrong ones. He no longer thought and spoke, "I need a drink." Instead he thinks and speaks, "I am a new creation in Christ." Not only does he think it, he constantly reinforces his victory by giving his testimony at every opportunity. He has not had a drop of alcohol to drink since. And he never went through "withdrawal" from alcohol. He simply reset his mind.

You can identify people with an unrenewed attitude by the way they talk, walk, shake hands, and the expression on their faces. If wrong thoughts and wrong friends control them, if their actions don't seem right, if their words lack faith and enthusiasm, then you know their minds are not renewed.

But people who allow God to renew their minds are full of faith, confidence, warmth, and stability. They light up a room with their presence and have fresh and exuberant personalities. They seem more "real" than other people. They have good perspectives on their own shortcomings and are convinced God is renewing those parts of their minds that need it day by day.

NEW PERSPECTIVE

Sometimes you need a change of perspective to help choose the proper input over the improper input. Changing how you see something can drastically change the conclusions that you draw.

At a baseball game some years ago, a man was drinking a soda. He started to have sharp pains in his stomach. He went to the concession stand and accused them of poisoning his drink. They called an ambulance and rushed him to the hospital. Meanwhile, the announcer spoke over the public address system and said, "Ladies and gentlemen, the concession stand will be closed for the rest of the game. A man was taken to the hospital because his soft drink may have been poisoned."

Immediately following this ill-advised announcement, hundreds of people started having stomach cramps, dizziness, and fainting. Scores of people had to be taken to the hospital.

The man who had first experienced stomach pains and leaped to the conclusion that he had been poisoned was examined by doctors. What did they find? He was suffering from gas! There was absolutely no poison involved. However, hundreds of perfectly healthy people told themselves that they also felt bad and had drunk poison. Their perspective changed, but in the wrong direction! That is a demonstration of the amazing power of the mind to draw wrong conclusions from wrong input.

I know of a little girl who really did drink poison one day. The bottle she drank from read: "Fatal If Swallowed." When her parent's discovered what she had done, they were terrified. But then they remembered, as born again Christians, they had promises to claim in this situation. Immediately, they began to act out of faith. Instead of speaking the worst outcome— death—they spoke the best outcome—life! Instead of reading the bottle and saying, "She's going to die! The bottle says so," they laid hands on their little girl and prayed, "The Word of God says if you drink any deadly thing it shall not hurt you. We claim that promise for our little girl."

They took her to the hospital, and the poison did not have one adverse effect on her. Today she is a healthy and happy young lady.

FACT VERSUS TRUTH

That is what happens when you carefully examine the input and change your perspective on what is true. The facts of a situation and the truth of a situation can be two very different things. The fact of the matter in this story was that the girl drank poison. But God's truth in this situation was...

...if they drink any deadly thing, it shall not hurt them; they shall lay hands on the sick, and they shall recover.

—Mark 16:18b

God's truth has the power to change facts.

I am reminded of the boy who went into the backyard with his baseball and bat. He said, "I am the greatest baseball player in the entire world." He tossed the ball into the air and swung at it with his bat—and missed. He repeated, "I am the greatest baseball player in the entire world." He tossed up the ball, swung, and missed again. A third time he said, "I am the greatest baseball player in the entire world," tossed up the ball, swung, and missed once more. After the third time of hitting nothing but air, he paused, thought for a moment and said, "Struck him out in three. Wow! What a pitcher!" Here was a boy who knew how to change his perspective!

One of history's most important discoveries was the vaccine for smallpox. Doctors had studied people stricken with this deadly disease for a long time but couldn't find a way of treating it, and most people who got smallpox died. Then Edward Jenner said, "Instead of studying people who have smallpox, let's study the people who aren't getting the disease and find out why they aren't."

He discovered that people who regularly milked cows seemed to be immune from smallpox, but that all of them who were immune had suffered a case of the much milder cowpox virus. Cowpox was no threat whatsoever, but it somehow gave them immunity to the much more deadly smallpox.

From that discovery, a vaccination based on cowpox was developed, and smallpox was stopped in its tracks. It took a change of perspective to save millions of lives.

BAD RELIGION

Sometimes a wrong perspective comes from religious beliefs. Fifteen-year old Butch did not know that he was too young to start a Bible study. As a member of Calvary Chapel in Costa Mesa, California, he took God at his Word. Soon his Thursday night Bible study grew so big he had to rent a room at the local synagogue. The insight God gave Butch of the Scriptures was phenomenal.

One evening, a woman came up to him and requested prayer for her eye. Butch laid hands on her and said, "Father, I pray for her eye."

She said, "You don't understand. This is a glass eye."

Well, nobody had ever told Butch that God couldn't heal a glass eye, so he continued, "I pray that she will be able to see out of this eye, even though it is glass."

The woman went home that night and her eye socket began to burn and itch. She removed her glass eye, and there was a new eye beginning to grow. Over the course of a few weeks it became a fully functioning, seeing eyeball that looked identical to her other one!

Butch had never been told that God could recreate an eyeball—but that didn't stop him from believing God could.

It amazes me how doubt, a product of the unrenewed mind, can neutralize faith, which is a product of the spirit. Jesus told us to have faith and doubt not!

> **Then Jesus told them, "I tell you the truth, if you have faith and don't doubt, you can do things like this and much more. You can even say to this mountain, 'May you be lifted up and thrown into the sea,' and it will happen."**
> **—Matthew 21:21 (NLT)**

Essentially, what he said was don't allow your mind to block what your spirit wants to do.

Religion is a tough thing to overcome. All my life, I've heard "religious" sayings like:

- "God gets the glory out of poverty. That is why godly people make vows of poverty."
- "Sickness is designed to teach you something. God gets glory out of your suffering."
- "It's God's will for you to be sick and poor."
- "Your sickness is a thorn in your flesh from God like Paul had."
- "Your purpose in life is to be like Job and suffer so that your patience is developed."

I bought into these so-called words of comfort and wisdom, until one day I picked up the Bible and started searching God's Word regarding these issues. I discovered that "religious tradition" had blocked my ability to renew my mind. Jesus told the Pharisees,

> **And so you cancel the word of God in order to hand down your own tradition.**
> **—Mark 7:13a (NLT)**

Later in this chapter he said,

> **15-16 The food that you put into your mouth doesn't make you unclean and unfit to worship God. The bad words that come out of your mouth are what make you unclean.**
> **—Mark 7:15–16 (CEV)**

I stopped telling myself that sickness and poverty were good, and my life has dramatically changed as a result. I no longer tell myself perverse things that don't match up to God's Word. He has helped me renew my mind in these areas.

RENOVATION

The Bible talks about the constant progression necessary to renew your mind, meaning it is a day-by-day process. Renewing your mind is like changing diapers. You must do it regularly—sometimes hourly—and it requires not just putting on a new one but taking off the old one first.

Some people want the new diaper—but they just want to put it on over the old one! Once, during an evangelistic meeting at our church, a man approached the evangelist and said, "I have eight demons in me and I would like you to cast five of them out."

The evangelist asked, "What about the other three demons?"

"I kind of want to keep those," he replied.

He wanted part of the new, but he also wanted to hang on to part of the old. That's not how God works. I see many believers who want to hold on to the old nature while at the same time embracing the new. I think that's why there are bald Christians. They come to the altar every Sunday and want someone to lay hands on them and pray, but they do not take up the daily task of renewing their minds. They come forward so often that the hair gets worn off the top of their heads! They are looking for a spiritual "shazam" moment—an instant, complete renewal with no effort on their part.

Renewing the mind is like renovating a house. The structure remains the same, but the inside looks very different. Once, Mary Jo and I went to a pizza parlor called "The Roaring Twenties." One of the kids in our youth group worked there. We had a great time and visited with the young man. Some time later, we went into the same place, but it had a new name: "The Royal Fork." Now it was a buffet-style restaurant, and we couldn't even recognize one thing about the place because the new owners had totally renovated the building.

As you become more like Christ through the renewing of your mind, your life and your very countenance will get a makeover. The structure will be the same, but the contents will be different. People will say, "That sure looks like Jennifer, but I can barely tell it's her. She looks so full of life and peace." Then you can tell them about your "renovation."

Renovation must come from the inside out. The restaurant we went back to had changed because it was under new ownership. Your life, too, should show signs of new ownership. The new owner of your life is Jesus Christ, who lives inside of you now. If renovation was an outside job—and I assumed I could make myself better without any help from God—the renovation would not last.

In New York City, there was a rundown housing project that caused many complaints. Finally, a group of Christians from the community decided to raise money to fix it up. They renovated the structures, put on fresh paint and wallpaper, scrubbed the bricks clean of dirt and graffiti, picked up garbage, planted flowers, and put in a lawn. Two years later the graffiti was back, the building was surrounded by garbage, the wallpaper and paint were dirty and scarred. Why? Because they did not change the thinking of the tenants who lived in that project, thus no permanent change could be maintained. They did an outside job, but not an inside job. Until the inside is changed, outward changes will only be temporary. It is true that your inner kingdom becomes your outer kingdom.

In the next chapter, we're going to look at four of the most life-changing principles that will make permanent renovations to our minds.

Your mind is a battlefield; determine to guard yours!

CHAPTER 7

STEPS TO SUCCESS

How do you develop right thinking? Let's see what the Bible has to say.

> Don't copy the behavior and customs of this world, but let God transform you into a new person by changing the way you think. Then you will learn to know God's will for you, which is good and pleasing and perfect.
>
> —Romans 12:2 (NLT)

And in Ephesians:

> ²¹ Since you have heard about Jesus and have learned the truth that comes from him,
>
> ²² throw off your old sinful nature and your former way of life, which is corrupted by lust and deception.
>
> ²³ Instead, let the Spirit renew your thoughts and attitudes.
>
> ²⁴ Put on your new nature, created to be like God— truly righteous and holy.
>
> —Ephesians 4:21–24 (NLT)

How do we accomplish this on a daily basis? There are four steps to take that I consider absolutely critical in your mind's renewal process.

First: Know the Truth

This may sound simple, but many people are deceived and don't know it. They think they know the truth when really they only know *about* the truth. Many people know about Jesus and about the Bible...but how many really know who he is and what the Bible says?

Here are just a few of the misconceptions I've heard regarding Jesus and the Bible.

I've heard, "God helps those who help themselves." Many people would tell you this saying is from the Bible, but it is not. Nowhere in the pages of the Bible will you find a phrase even similar to that. However, many people accept it as a biblical "truth." They have never bothered to check this folksy "truism" against the source—God's Word.

Most Americans claim to be Christians, but only a small fraction of them probably have a real relationship with Jesus. Many seem to think that the rights and privileges of a child of God are automatically theirs as citizens of the United States of America. Others seem to think that truth will hunt them down in a time of trouble and deliver them, superhero-style, from their enemies. These kinds of people quote the Scripture that says, "The truth will set me free," but that is not what Scripture says. Jesus said:

> ³¹ **Jesus said to the people who believed in him, "You are truly my disciples if you remain faithful to my teachings.**
>
> ³² **And you will know the truth, and the truth will set you free."**
>
> **—John 8:31–32 (NLT)**

Before the truth can set you free you must make an effort to know the truth! Most people would rather claim that the truth would set them free, rather that make the effort to get acquainted with the truth.

How do you know the truth? By accepting Jesus as your Savior and developing a relationship with him, you will begin to know the truth. Once you have established that salvation relationship, you want to grow and deepen that relationship and you need to constantly remind yourself of what is true. You do that by studying the Bible, going to a good, Bible-based church, listening to Christian worship and teaching audio programs, watching Christian video programs, reading godly books, and developing friendships with other mature Christians. Anything that reminds you, teaches you, and prods you toward the truth is useful for the renewing of your mind.

I cannot count the number of times I've read the Bible through from Genesis to Revelation. I have read the New Testament even more times. Why? Because there is a battle going on for the dominion of my mind, and I want God's will and way to have the power over my mind.

> **3 For though we walk in the flesh, we do not war after the flesh:**
>
> **4 (For the weapons of our warfare are not carnal, but mighty through God to the pulling down of strong holds;)**
>
> **5 Casting down imaginations, and every high thing that exalteth itself against the knowledge of God, and bringing into captivity every thought to the obedience of Christ....**
>
> **—2 Corinthians 10:3–5**

THE BIGGEST BATTLEGROUND: YOUR MIND

The greatest battle you and I will ever face is the battle waged for the domination of our minds. I am determined to guard my mind carefully; you should guard yours too. Recently, I talked with a woman who had accepted Jesus as her Savior. As we talked, I realized she was more spiritually mature than many preachers I know. I commented, "You must have been brought up in the church."

She replied, "No, I've only been saved four years, but when I got saved I immediately started taking Bible study courses."

This woman made a deliberate, concentrated effort to know the truth—and the truth set her spirit, mind, and body free. So…first, know the truth.

Second: Think the Truth

Thinking the truth is like watering a lawn. The water seeps down into the soil and makes contact with the roots. When you dwell on God's Word, the truth goes into the conscious and subconscious parts of your mind. You ingest the truth; it becomes a part of you. If you know the truth but do not dwell on it, you will have a weak root system and be like the seeds in Jesus' parable of the sower:

> **5 Some fell upon stony places, where they had not much earth: and forthwith they sprung up, because they had no deepness of earth:**
>
> **6 And when the sun was up, they were scorched; and because they had no root, they withered away.**
>
> **—Matthew 13:5–6**

You need to live with the Word of God, return to it daily, think about it, ponder it, and meditate upon it. Ask the Holy

Spirit to reveal its deepest meanings to you. When you do this, it becomes a part of the very fabric of your being; you will have an intimate knowledge of God's Word.

Later, we will study the lost art of meditation in greater detail. For now, it is important to understand that simply knowing the truth and having some information will not help you nearly as much as filling your mind with it day by day.

Third: Speak the Truth

Your mind loves the sound of your own voice. Your mind loves to believe what you say. When you say something, it becomes your truth—even if what you say is false. There is tremendous power in the spoken word.

Your mind and your mouth are accustomed to repeating bad news. Our fallen world has conditioned you to believe that bad news is the norm. Murphy's Law states that if anything can go wrong, it will. The reason that statement is so popular is because it bears witness to the unrenewed mind.

And when you speak Murphy's Law, you speak defeat into your own life. Numbers, chapter thirteen, relates an example of how men's words thwarted God's plan for his people. God had brought the Israelites to the land of Canaan. He told Moses that this was the land he was giving to the Israelites for their new home. So, Moses called leaders from each of the twelve tribes to go into Canaan and explore the land. When the men came back from their explorations they reported of a land rich and fertile—a land flowing with milk and honey. But they had other things to report as well:

> **28 But the people living there are powerful, and their towns are large and fortified. We even saw giants there, the descendants of Anak!**

²⁹ The Amalekites live in the Negev, and the Hittites, Jebusites, and Amorites live in the hill country. The Canaanites live along the coast of the Mediterranean Sea and along the Jordan Valley."

³⁰ But Caleb tried to quiet the people as they stood before Moses. "Let's go at once to take the land," he said. "We can certainly conquer it!"

³¹ But the other men who had explored the land with him disagreed. "We can't go up against them! They are stronger than we are!"

³² So they spread this bad report about the land among the Israelites: "The land we traveled through and explored will devour anyone who goes to live there. All the people we saw were huge.

³³ We even saw giants there, the descendants of Anak. Next to them we felt like grasshoppers, and that's what they thought, too!"

—Numbers 13:28–33 (NLT)

Only Caleb and Joshua spoke words of courage and faith in God's plan. They were the only ones who boldly urged the Israelites to step out in faith.

⁶ Two of the men who had explored the land, Joshua son of Nun and Caleb son of Jephunneh, tore their clothing.

⁷ They said to all the people of Israel, "The land we traveled through and explored is a wonderful land!

⁸ And if the LORD is pleased with us, he will bring us safely into that land and give it to us. It is a rich land flowing with milk and honey.

⁹ Do not rebel against the LORD, and don't be afraid of the people of the land. They are only helpless prey to us! They have no protection, but the LORD is with us! Don't be afraid of them!"

—Numbers 14:6–9 (NLT)

What was the result of the Israelites disobedience and fear? They were condemned to wander for another forty years in the desert. The faithless words the men reported spread throughout the camp, and the people gladly believed the worst and continued to speak it. "I knew it! We never should have gotten our hopes up. We will lose too much if we try to take that land. Forget it!"

YOUR WORDS DECIDE YOUR FUTURE

They embraced Murphy's Law with a vengeance, and the words they spoke were directly opposed to the promises God had given them. Their spoken words—negative words— played a critical role in deciding their future.

The easiest thing in the world to do is to think and speak the worst. But the power of life and death is in the tongue. [1] Proverbs says that the tongue of the wise is health. [2] Why not get up in the morning and instead of saying, "It's going to be one of those days," say, "This is the day that the Lord has made. I will rejoice and be glad in it. [3] Today, something good is going to happen to me!"

Your mind and spirit will jump for joy!

Only speak words that are in harmony with God's Word. An unspoken thought will die. When the devil whispers in your ear, "You're depressed," do not speak those words out loud. Do not even entertain the thought in your mind, and it will die. When you speak a thought out loud, it grows and

---

[1] Death and life are in the power of the tongue: and they that love it shall eat the fruit thereof. —Proverbs 18:21

[2] There is that speaketh like the piercings of a sword: but the tongue of the wise is health. —Proverbs 12:18

[3] This is the day which the LORD hath made; we will rejoice and be glad in it. —Psalm 118:24

becomes real. The more we talk about God's promises, the bigger and more real they grow.

Fourth: Act on the Truth

This is called being a hypocrite in reverse. In the Greek, a *hypocrite* is an actor, someone who pretends to be something he is not. Maybe you don't always feel like your mind is being renewed—but the truth is the truth; God is renewing your mind no matter what your feelings tell you. You must believe what the Bible says to believe in spite of what you might feel at any particular moment, what your circumstances might seem to dictate, or what other people are telling you. You must believe God's Word above anything else at all.

The Bible says:

- We have joy unspeakable and are filled with glory. [4]
- The Kingdom of God is not meat and drink; but righteousness, peace, and joy in the Holy Ghost. [5]

These statements are the truth even when you don't feel like they are true, and when you act on these statements they become your reality. Each time you act on the truth, another little place in your mind has been renewed. If you do not act on the truth, your mind will not be renewed.

In Grand Rapids, Michigan, there is a very old Dutch Reformed Church that used to be stodgy and lifeless. The oldest member in the church could not even remember the last time someone accepted Christ as his or her Savior. But God had something great planned for this church.

---

[4] ...though now ye see him not, yet believing, ye rejoice with joy unspeakable and full of glory.... —1 Peter 1:8

[5] Romans 14:17

One day the pastor, "Sam," was flying back from a conference. In the seat next to him was Pastor Larry of the First Assembly of God in Grand Rapids. They began to talk, and Larry told Sam about the revival that was sweeping through First Assembly.

Sam had never been in a charismatic service, and he did not know what being "born again" meant. Larry told him stories of people repenting of their sins and being healed. Sam's interest was sparked. He had never seen anyone come to Christ. He had never seen miracles happen in his church. Maybe there was something to this.

The next Friday night, he went to a service at Grand Rapids First Assembly and saw things he had never seen before: people were dancing before the Lord, lifting their hands, worshiping God freely, weeping, and laying prostrate before the altar. Something deep inside Sam felt the people's genuine love for God and the intimate relationship these people had with him.

The evangelist speaking that night said he wanted to pray for pastors. Sam was faced with a choice. Should he go down front and risk being recognized? What if nothing happened and he felt like a fool?

After a few moments of indecision, he decided he wanted to really know God. He got out of his seat and went forward for prayer. When one of the pastors laid hands on him and prayed for him, Sam went down under the power of the Holy Spirit. Nothing like that had ever happened to him before. Forty-five minutes later, he was still on the floor. He began to ask for Pastor Larry, because he didn't know anyone else there. An usher brought Pastor Larry over and Sam asked, "How long am I going to be down here?"

"The last time I was in that position it lasted about two-and-a-half hours," Larry responded.

After awhile, Sam got up and began praying in a heavenly language. He told Larry, "I cannot wait to get back to my own church!"

On Saturday he visited the chief lay leader in his church and told him what had happened to him at First Assembly. The elder looked at him and said, "Pastor, I've been sneaking over to First Assembly on Friday nights myself!"

That Sunday, Sam stepped into the pulpit and preached like he was hearing words from another world. He told the people they must be born again. He gave his first altar call and the altar was packed with people wanting to know Jesus as their Savior. Then he pulled out a bottle of oil and said, "Now we're going to anoint the sick and pray for healing." They began to anoint the sick and God started healing people.

Needless to say, that church has never been the same. It isn't staid and stodgy anymore.

The reason I tell you this story is because the pastor did something very bold. He not only changed his mind about what he believed—he acted on it. If he had simply held on to the knowledge and pondered it, people would not have been saved or healed.

When you act on the truth, you begin to see remarkable, miraculous, supernatural things happen in your life.

These four principles...

- Know the truth
- Think the truth
- Speak the truth
- Act on the truth

...are perhaps the most important principles you will ever learn. It would be impossible to overstate their value to you as a believer. These principles are the foundation of everything

Jesus performed in his ministry when he walked the earth. They are instilled in everything his disciples accomplished in their ministry before and after Jesus went to Heaven. Every notable action or achievement by any man or woman of God in the Bible firmly rested on these four bedrock principles.

There is another way to get the most out of your mind's power. Let's investigate this important method next.

Meditating on God's promises as found in his Word takes the
"nutrients" out of the book and implants them inside you.

CHAPTER 8

THE LOST ART OF MEDITATION

Is there a way that the promises found in the Bible can be ingrained into your mind? Is it possible to make God's truth a part of the very fabric of your being? Yes, and it happens in large measure through the lost art of meditation.

WHAT MEDITATION ISN'T

As Christians, we recoil from the term "meditation" because it has been stolen and improperly used by demonic religions and practitioners of Hindu-like meditation. The word brings to mind images of a swami sitting lotus-style on a pillow on the side of a mountain or a class full of yoga students trying to find inner peace. However, genuine meditation is a beautiful biblical concept found in the Old and New Testaments and has nothing to do with the occult practices with which it has come to be associated.

I knew a Sunday school teacher who was well loved by his church. He could expound on Scriptures in an extraordinary way. Then he started experimenting with transcendental meditation. He said he wasn't practicing a religion, he was just using it as a stress reliever. He thought that by picturing colors in his mind and repeating a mantra he could alleviate his stress.

People tried to tell him it would harm his walk with the Lord, but he did not listen. One day, during meditation, a voice spoke to him and told him he had married the wrong woman. So, he left his wife and family and moved in with an old sweetheart.

As he discovered, this was not a harmless stress reliever but an occult practice that soon stirred up demonic forces that caused him to lose his ministry, his family, and his walk with the true and living God.

Genuine, biblical meditation is not opening up your spirit to false voices, as that man did. Neither is daydreaming the same as biblical meditation. Meditation isn't trying to discover some "deeper" or "hidden" meaning in a Scripture by over-spiritualizing or reading more into it than is actually there.

I know of a man who rewrote the book of Revelation because God had "revealed" new meanings to him during a time of meditation. This man claimed that he, like the Apostle John, was caught up into heaven and was given the "true" explanation of the book of Revelation. He bought television time and propounded on his wacky, senseless ideas.

Meditation does not mean reading a Scripture and then finding a "truth" in it that nobody else knows.

WHAT MEDITATION IS

Every successful, happy Christian I know makes meditation a daily part of his or her walk with the Lord. The Bible says...

For as he thinketh in his heart, so is he....

—Proverbs 23:7a

The Hebrew word for "thinketh" paints a picture of letting something come in through a gateway. Here it means opening the gate of your mind to God's Word. The thoughts you allow to go through the "gateway" of your mind literally write your future. Your inner reality creates your outer reality.

The Hebrew word for "meditate" means to repeat aloud over and over, to digest. It essentially means to speak the Word of God, which is outside of you, until the Holy Spirit, who is living inside of you, explains it to you.

All of us meditate on something. When you're running errands, standing in line at the bank, or sitting in your car at a stoplight your mind is thinking about something. What thoughts do you allow to engage your mind?

Have you ever caught yourself thinking about something you don't really want to consider? Do you find yourself worrying? Do you think about problems, or do you meditate on solutions? Your meditations play a monumental role in what your life is like. Remember, success starts in the mind. If you meditate on success, your spirit, mind, and body focus in that direction. Jesus said,

> **"What do you mean, 'If I can'?" Jesus asked.**
> **"Anything is possible if a person believes."**
> **—Mark 9:23 (NLT)**

That means with the right input, with the right meditations, you shape your future. If you meditate on God's truth, the future will be the one he has planned for you, and it will be filled with good things.

> **[10] This is what the LORD says: "You will be in Babylon for seventy years. But then I will come and do for you all the good things I have promised, and I will bring you home again.**

> [11] "For I know the plans I have for you," says the
> LORD. "They are plans for good and not for disaster,
> to give you a future and a hope."
>
> —Jeremiah 29:10–11 (NLT)

If you meditate on God's promises, they tend to become reality in your life. If you think about succeeding, you will. If you think about problems, then problems become your reality. If you think about failing, you will fail. Your inner "kingdom" will eventually become your outer "kingdom."

MEDITATE DAY AND NIGHT

Where do you find this principle in the Bible? Begin with Joshua, chapter one, where God told Joshua how to be a success.

> [7] Only be thou strong and very courageous, that
> thou mayest observe to do according to all the law,
> which Moses my servant commanded thee: turn not
> from it to the right hand or to the left, that thou may-
> est prosper withersoever thou goest.
>
> [8] This book of the law shall not depart out of thy
> mouth; but thou shalt meditate therein day and night,
> that thou mayest observe to do according to all that
> is written therein: for then thou shalt make thy way
> prosperous, and then thou shalt have good success.
>
> —Joshua 1:7–8

Notice the phrases "meditate therein day and night," and "thou shalt make thy way prosperous." Here God inextricably links meditation with success. If you meditate on God's Word, you will be enabled to act and live in such a way that you draw to yourself success and prosperity.

Here are more verses that reinforce this point:

> [1] Blessed is the man that walketh not in the counsel
> of the ungodly, nor standeth in the way of sinners, nor
> sitteth in the seat of the scornful.

> [2] But his delight is in the law of the LORD; and in his law doth he meditate day and night.
>
> —Psalm 1:1–2

> Meditate upon these things; give thyself wholly to them; that thy profiting may appear to all.
>
> —1 Timothy 4:15

Some Christians don't want to learn to meditate because they think it's too much work. They would rather think about the stock market, sports, their "to-do" list, their next pay raise, or anything other than the things important to God. And yet, they carry around a Bible thinking it will give them some kind of "magical" protection. I've heard unspiritual people say things like, "If anything bad happens, I'll just hold up my Bible for protection."

The devil laughs at such people because the physical Bible—the book made from paper and ink—has no power in and of itself. It only becomes powerful when it gets inside your mind, is absorbed into your spirit and becomes a part of you. That's when God's power can be released into your situation. Meditating on God's promises as found in his Word takes the "nutrients" out of the book and implants them inside of you.

You could take a piece of juicy steak and a loaf of bread and tie them by a string around your neck, but would that food nourish your body? Of course it wouldn't! It won't strengthen and nourish your body until you put it in your mouth, chew it up and swallow it. The same is true of the cross around your neck or the Bible in your hand. They have no power to change your situation or protect you. God's Word is not some magic amulet like you see in fantasy movies or video games. The power in the Bible is spiritual power and it must connect with your spirit for you to reap any benefit. When you read a Scripture, reread it, speak it, re-speak it, and think about it throughout the day until your spirit digests it and it becomes part of you.

DIGESTING THE WORD

There are types of grazing animals called ruminants; these animals have four stomachs, and cows belong to this group. When a cow takes a bite of grass, chews and swallows it, the food goes into the first stomach. Stomach number one stores the grass and gradually passes it into the second stomach where microorganisms begin to break the grass down. From there the "cud" comes back up the esophagus and the cow chews it some more. Then the cud is again swallowed and goes into stomach number three, and from there it goes to the fourth stomach. By the time this process is finished, every bit of nourishment has been wrung out of that grass and has become part of the cow.

This is an illustration of biblical meditation. All the nutrients, vitamins, minerals, enzymes, proteins—everything you need to stay spiritually healthy—become part of you when you digest God's word through meditation. Just like cows "burp" up food, we should be "burping" up Scriptures. Start chewing on a little piece and take it into your spiritual "stomach." Burp it up again, chew on it some more, and continue this process until every bit of goodness and faith from that Scripture becomes part of you.

Soon that Scripture will be completely digested. You will have wisdom and insight because of it. That is how the Word becomes flesh in us.

Have you ever pondered a certain Scripture, only to have its meaning dawn on you weeks or months later? It happens to me. Sometimes I think about a passage of Scripture for years. I turn it over in my mind, letting it sit in my spirit. One day, out of the clear blue, it hits me: "So that's what it means!" God gives me insight after I've meditated on his Word for a while.

This happens to me even with Scriptures that I thought I understood. God shows it to me in a different light and gives me fresh insight and revelation.

It is better to be a river than a swamp. A river flows and moves; a swamp spreads out. Those who do not meditate tend to drift from here to there without focus or logic—and they can drift into big trouble.

CHAPTER 9

WHAT YOU GAIN

Amazing results come when you learn the lost art of meditation and when your mind is enriched with the promises of God. Let's look at four things you will gain.

Number One: Success

The Hebrew word for "success" means to have favorable results. Remember what God said in Joshua:

> **This book of the law shall not depart out of thy mouth; but thou shalt meditate therein day and night, that thou mayest observe to do according to all that is written therein: for then thou shalt make thy way prosperous, and then thou shalt have good success.**
>
> **—Joshua 1:8**

A young man joined the army as a private. It did not take long before he noticed there was a difference between an enlisted man and an officer, and he decided he did not always want to be an enlisted man.

He started dreaming about becoming an officer. He began meditating on the uniform he would wear and thinking about what it would feel like to put on a commissioned officer's uniform instead of a private's uniform. He discovered an Army program in which he could complete his college degree while taking officer training. He worked hard and the day finally arrived. He graduated from officer's training, received his commission, and became a second lieutenant. Today he is a colonel, ready to retire from the Army. His successful military career began with meditation.

George is a well-known mathematician. When he was in college, he came late to class one day. There were two problems on the chalkboard plus a take-home exam. He wrote down the problems from the chalkboard, went back to his apartment, and started meditating on them. He completed the exam with little difficulty, but the two problems from the chalkboard were tougher. One of them he couldn't figure out at all. The other one he worked on all night, meditating on it and writing down ideas. The next day, he turned his answers in to the professor.

The next night, he heard someone banging on his door. When he opened it, he saw his professor standing there. Thinking his teacher was there about his incomplete test paper he said, "I'm sorry. I just couldn't get that other problem."

"Forget about that," answered his professor. "You were late for class. Before you came, I told the class there are some problems and equations that cannot be solved. Even Einstein couldn't solve those two problems. I wrote them on the chalkboard to encourage the class, and you solved one of them."

The school immediately awarded George a full scholarship to complete his PhD, and when he finished, he landed a career that paid hundreds of thousands of dollars a year. Today, he is one of the foremost mathematicians in the world.

These two examples are in a secular context, but the same principle applies to believers. How much more can you achieve by meditating on godly things and allowing God's solutions, directly from his Word, to permeate your life.

Number Two: Prosperity

When I was a boy, my friends and I would take a magnifying glass and let the sun focus through it onto piles of leaves and start little fires. The sun alone, without being focused, would not be able to set those leaves on fire. But we had a tool that focused the sun's energy.

Meditation is such a tool. You use it to focus your thoughts on success. You can accomplish a hundred to a thousand times more in your life when you are focused. Success follows the one who is focused!

MEDITATION LEADS TO MILLIONS

Rob was in his third year of undergraduate studies in nuclear physics when he realized that by the time he finished graduate school, there would be no demand for nuclear physicists. He became depressed and dropped out of college. His father, who ran an insurance business, wanted to help him. He said, "Rob, come and design a computer program that will help me serve our customers better." Rob set his mind to develop such a program.

He thought about it day and night. When he went to bed he would pray, "Lord, what about doing this? Do you think that would work?" He would wake up with his head filled with ideas. After six months he completed the computer program. It was such an effective and well-written program that his father marketed it to other insurance companies. They became so successful that in five years they sold the insurance software side of the business for forty million dollars!

What began as a setback in Rob's education was really an open door, and he meditated on their software problem long

71

enough that he completely digested the problem and came up with a solution that financially blessed his entire family.

RIVER OR SWAMP?

It is better to be a river than a swamp. A river flows and moves; a swamp spreads out all over the place. Those who do not meditate tend to drift from here to there without focus or logic—and they can drift into big trouble. Their minds are untrained and unfocused. They bounce back and forth from the television to the refrigerator to the telephone to a book. They let external factors determine their schedules. They spread themselves all over the place like a swamp. A swamp has no force or direction, but a river has great force. A swamp is spread out; a river is focused.

Number Three: Stability

In Psalms you find a wonderful promise of fruitfulness to those who meditate on God's Word.

> ¹ **Blessed is the man that walketh not in the counsel of the ungodly, nor standeth in the way of sinners, nor sitteth in the seat of the scornful.**
> ² **But his delight is in the law of the LORD; and in his law doth he meditate day and night.**
> ³ **And he shall be like a tree planted by the rivers of water, that bringeth forth his fruit in his season; his leaf also shall not wither; and whatsoever he doeth shall prosper.**
>
> **—Psalm 1:1–3**

The Word says you will be blessed like a tree planted by the water—always fruitful. We have all known Christians who are up and down, in and out. I have heard them say, "I'm going to the prayer meeting. Glory to God! This is the greatest thing in the world." It seems like they have everything going for them, but the next week they are not in church. The next time you see them they say, "I just didn't feel like coming."

It's easy to identify people who do not meditate on God's Word because they have no stability. They experience things on the surface, but nothing is being digested and internalized.

Ron went to Heaven a few years ago, but even in his nineties he would regularly call me from Delaware where he had moved to be near his son and daughter. Ron was a member of my church for many years, but back in the "Roaring '20s" he was the youngest member of a gangster mob. He was arrested, tried, and went to prison for 17 years. In his cell there was only one thing to read—a Gideon Bible. He happened to read John, chapter three, and kept reading it. He asked himself, what does this mean? Then something happened. John 3:16 began to light up like neon lights. It began to flash; only this time it said:

"For God so loved Ron, that he gave his only begotten Son, that if Ron believeth in him Ron should not perish, but have everlasting life."

Ron went from being a sinner to a saint in that moment. His meditation yielded results. After his release from prison, he established a prison ministry at our church, and it became the finest prison ministry in the state, serving twenty-six different correctional facilities. On Sunday mornings, people from our church lead services in prisons all over the state.

Ron is the picture of a stable Christian whose labor yields long-lasting results. Though he is now in Heaven, the work he established at our church is still growing and causing people to be saved and helped.

Number Four: Wisdom

Psalm 119 says that through meditation you will gain wisdom greater than your enemies.

> [97] **O how love I thy law! it is my meditation all the day.**
>
> [98] **Thou through thy commandments hast made me wiser than mine enemies: for they are ever with me.**
>
> [99] **I have more understanding than all my teachers: for thy testimonies are my meditation.**
>
> [100] **I understand more than the ancients, because I keep thy precepts.**
>
> **—Psalm 119:97–100**

EXCEL ABOVE THE CROWD

Do you want wisdom that soars above the crowd? Do you want to excel above people who hate you or try to sabotage your success at work or church or anywhere else?

Then meditate! This passage says you will gain more understanding than your teachers and all the wisest people in history.

Those who say, "I do not have time to meditate," have sliced and diced their chance to gain wisdom, success, prosperity, and stability. Don't you think it's time you learned this valuable skill?

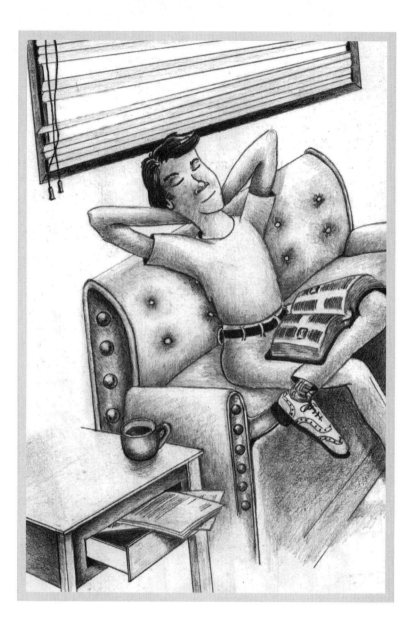

Be willing to wait on the Lord.

10
CHAPTER

HOW TO MEDITATE
IN A BIBLICAL WAY

Now that you know what you gain through meditating on God's Word, you need to know how to do it. Here are five simple steps that will make meditation a powerful tool in your life.

Number One: Be Willing to Wait on the Lord

Our lives seem to be infected by a spirit of hurry. I am no stranger to this phenomenon. Each day, I have my plan—my schedule. I know what I'm doing at two o'clock, three o'clock, etc. I am organized and goal-oriented. I work long hours and know exactly what I want to accomplish in those hours. Sometimes when it's time to sit before the Lord, a spirit of hurry presses on me. I think of all the "things" I am not accomplishing because I'm "just sitting."

That thought is a meditation killer. Waiting is a critical first step towards effective meditation on God's Word. I have learned to block off those times and not let anything, especially my own thoughts, get in the way. If I think of something important, I write it down and set it aside so I can deal with it later.

The Bible promises that they who wait on the Lord will renew their strength, mount up with wings as eagles, run and not be weary, walk and not grow faint.

> **But they that wait upon the LORD shall renew their strength; they shall mount up with wings as eagles; they shall run, and not be weary; and they shall walk, and not faint.**
>
> **—Isaiah 40:31**

The Bible says in Genesis 24 that Isaac went out in the field to meditate.

> **And Isaac went out to meditate in the field at the eventide: and he lifted up his eyes, and saw, and, behold, the camels were coming.**
>
> **—Genesis 24:63**

So there was Isaac sitting in a field meditating. He looked into the distance and saw a caravan of camels coming toward him. A beautiful woman hopped off one of the camels, ran up to him and said, "Praise the Lord! You are to be my husband!"

Those are the kinds of surprises in store for you if you are willing to wait on the Lord.

Number Two: Take One Bite of Scripture at a Time

Mommies and daddies always tell their children to take small bites and chew their food well, and that is pretty good advice for meditating on the Scriptures. Your mind cannot think about a whole book of the Bible at one time. Most of us probably couldn't think about even one whole chapter. You need to break it down, line-by-line, thought-by-thought, and truth-by-truth. Context is important, so you need to read chapters or books in one sitting, but within the context you will discover many truths.

Choose a book of the Bible and begin to break it down. Read it through a couple of times and then start meditating on specific Scriptures. Maybe you will read Joshua 1:6–9 or Psalm 1. The Holy Spirit will guide you to the right place.

The disciples asked Jesus lots of questions and received bite-sized answers. That's probably one of the reasons Jesus had to be with them for three years. If their minds had been capable, Jesus could have "downloaded" all his truth in one sitting. But he knew that their minds could only absorb small amounts at a time. You are the same. You will be better able to take it in when you take it in small allotments.

Believe me, one "bite" of Scripture can be very filling! The better you digest it, the more power it will bring. Understanding even one single truth from the Bible can revolutionize your life.

Number Three: Read It Repeatedly...And Out Loud

This is how you transfer spiritual truth from the Word into your spirit. You read it out loud so your mind will hear it. By repeating it, your mind knows it is important and begins processing it.

The first thing that occurs to you when you face any situation, will be the focus of your meditations. If you meditate on money, you will always think about money first when a new situation arises. If you are meditating on finding a spouse, your mind will jump to that subject in every new circumstance. If you constantly meditate on God's Word, it will be readily available to you when you need it.

By reading something repeatedly and letting your ears hear your mouth say it, you reinforce what is important to you and cause it to leap to mind in new situations.

Number Four: View it From all Angles

Ask the Lord questions. "Lord, who, what, where, when, and why?" God's promises are like precious diamonds. You can examine them from all angles and see something different from every direction.

Meditation is about having a dialogue with God. He will answer your questions and give you insights as you examine his Word from all angles.

Number Five: Think About It Before You Go to Sleep

What do you want your mind to work on during the night while you are asleep? The thoughts you take to bed become your nighttime meditations. There are dozens of stories of men and women throughout history who solved major problems, or came up with dazzling new inventions, while they were sleeping. One of the most recorded songs of all time—*Yesterday*, by Paul McCartney—came to him while he was asleep. When he woke up, he rolled out of bed and started playing it on the piano.

Meditation is a powerful tool that God encourages you to use to center your focus on him, to understand his Word, and to focus your thoughts on specific goals. There is another tool God has given that most of us wish we could use more effectively.

Examine God's precious promises from all angles.

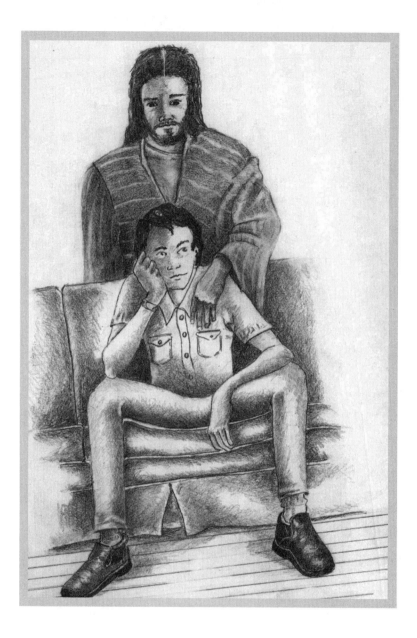

You can share in the mind of Christ!
The first step to having a great memory is having the faith to
believe that Jesus wants to share his mind with you.

11
CHAPTER

YOUR TERRIFIC MEMORY

How many times have you wished you had a better memory? Have you ever walked into a room...hmmm, why am I here? Have you left your keys someplace and have no idea where? Have you ever greeted someone at church and thought *I've met this guy five times before. Why can't I remember his name?* Have you ever...

- forgotten your wedding anniversary?
- forgotten an important birthday?
- forgotten to make a house payment?
- forgotten where you parked the car?
- forgotten where you put your glasses?

A certain pilot grew tired of landing on runways, so he put pontoons on his airplane so he could take off and land on the lake near his house. One day, he and his wife took off from the lake, flew around for a bit and decided to land at the airport for some coffee. As he was coming in for a landing, his wife said, "Honey, remember you have the pontoons on."

He yanked up the flaps, shoved the throttle forward, pulled back the yoke, and zoomed back up into the sky, narrowly averting disaster.

He landed on a lake close by, looked over at his wife and said, "I don't know what happened to me back there. I forgot all about having those pontoons on the plane." Then he stepped out the door and fell into the lake!

Once a woman asked her pastor, "Can you help me? I have this problem remembering things."

"How long have you had this problem?" he queried.

"What problem?" she asked.

We all have faced problems with our memories. These days, systems for improving your memory are big money makers. I have seen infomercials on how to develop a powerful mega-memory. There are literally hundreds of courses for sale because people understand the value of being able to remember names, dates, figures, and facts. Knowledge is power, and memory is where we store knowledge.

Science holds that everything you have ever experienced is recorded in your brain. That means that in a perfect world, you ought to remember everything—every detail, every word of everything you hear, see, say, and experience. God originally gave mankind perfect recall, but that ability was lost when Adam and Eve sinned in the Garden of Eden and fell from God's grace. Nevertheless, even though you might not have perfect recall, your ability to remember is a critical component of your spectacular mind that you must use effectively so the rest of your work will not be hindered.

BENEFITS OF GOOD MEMORY

There are many promises to be found in the Bible concerning memory.

> But thou shalt *remember* the LORD thy God: for it
> is he that giveth thee power to get wealth, that he may
> establish his covenant which he sware unto thy fathers,
> as it is this day.
>
> —Deuteronomy 8:18 (italics added)

God told Joshua...

> *Remember* the word which Moses the servant of the
> LORD commanded you, saying, The LORD your God
> hath *given* you rest, and hath *given* you this land.
>
> —Joshua 1:13 (italics added)

In the New Testament, Paul said...

> ¹ Moreover, brethren, I declare unto you the gospel
> which I preached unto you, which also ye have re-
> ceived, and wherein ye stand;
>
> ² By which also ye are saved, if ye *keep in memory*
> what I preached unto you, unless ye have believed in
> vain.
>
> —1 Corinthians 15:1–2 (italics added)

In Proverbs, you are promised long life and prosperity if
you remember God's teaching...

> ¹ My son, *forget not* my law; but let thine heart keep
> my commandments:
>
> ² For length of days, and long life, and peace, shall
> they add to thee.
>
> —Proverbs 3:1–2 (italics added)

Psalms also lists many benefits to those who do not forget
the Lord...

> ² Bless the LORD, O my soul, and *forget not all his
> benefits*:
>
> ³ Who forgiveth all thine iniquities; who healeth all
> thy diseases;

85

> ⁴ Who redeemeth thy life from destruction; who crowneth thee with lovingkindness and tender mercies;
>
> ⁵ Who satisfieth thy mouth with good things; so that thy youth is renewed like the eagle's.
>
> —Psalm 103:2–5 (italics added)

In James you can find another promise of blessings for those who remember what God's Word teaches...

> But whoever looks intently into the perfect law that gives freedom, and continues in it—*not forgetting* what they have heard, but doing it—they will be blessed in what they do..
>
> —James 1:25 (NIV, italics added)

Memory is like a file cabinet with manila folders organized into thousands of categories. When you hit thirty years of age, you have billions and billions of manila envelopes in your file cabinet, and it seems to take a little longer to find the file you want to open.

Most people believe their memories will worsen as they get older, and for most people that is true. However, this is not because memory has to degenerate over time. It becomes true when you fail to exercise your memory as you grow older. Your memory grows rusty from disuse. Memory is like a muscle. When you exercise your memory, it stays strong; when you fail to exercise your memory, it atrophies.

Frank Felberbaum was the first U.S. gold medalist at the 1995 World Memory Olympics, and is the President and CEO of Memory Training Systems. Over 200,000 business executives, government leaders, and educators have improved their memories and boosted brain performance using Felberbaum's techniques. In an interview he said, "Memory is an equal opportunity skill. Most people assume that their memory is as good as it gets and they don't think their memory can be trained or improved. I'm in the business of training memory. I have worked with people from nine to ninety years old, and any brain at any age can be shaped and molded by specific memory systems, techniques, and methods." [1]

He went on to say:

"I've been in the field almost thirty years, and I have never reached the plateau yet. The capacity for your ability to control and apply information is really unlimited. When people hit forty they think their memory is failing them, or going downhill, and in reality that's a myth. As we get older we should learn new languages, new skills, have interesting discussions, do puzzles…many people vegetate, and that is the worst thing you can do to your memory.

"When you improve your memory, all your other skills are enhanced. Communication, problem solving, ability to manage and supervise people, ability to market products, ability to provide good customer service. Just dealing with information in general is greatly enhanced, and you feel much more confident. You get the feeling that you know. There is nothing better than that. You have the competitive edge over everybody else because your memory is working for you on all eight cylinders."

The Bible tells you to remember a lot of things. In fact, lack of memory can get you into trouble. Psalm 9:17 says

---

1 Quotes by Frank Felberbaum taken from a live chat transcript, copyright © 2000, ABC News, Internet Ventures.

there will be judgment on any nation that forgets God. Romans 1:28 says that God gave up certain people to a reprobate mind because they did not like to retain the knowledge of God in their thinking. In Psalm 78 and Psalm 106 you are told that the children of Israel forgot certain things, and God's mercies stopped.

Why did God give you a memory?

Number One: To Remember God's Word

When Jesus went into the wilderness to fast for forty days, the devil came to try and defeat him at his lowest ebb. To combat the foe, Jesus needed to use the Word of God.

Think what would have happened if Jesus had not remembered what God's Word said. Human logic will not thwart the devil. But Jesus had sharpened both "edges" of his mind. He had meditated on the Word, allowing it to permeate his soul, and he had memorized it. When he said, "It is written: 'Man doth not live on bread only, but on every word that proceedeth out of the mouth of the LORD…' " (Matthew 4:4) he was quoting the Word perfectly [2] and with the force of conviction that comes from meditation.

Does memorization alone help you? No. In fact, nowhere in the Bible are we instructed to memorize Scripture. There is only one Scripture that is remotely related to memorization, and you have to stretch to give it that meaning.

> **Thy word have I hid in mine heart, that I might not sin against thee.**
>
> **—Psalm 119: 11**

But this verse is more about meditation than memorization. Meditating is closely associated with the ability to

---

[2] Deuteronomy 8:3

remember things. Memorization is important only insofar as it helps you internalize the Word of God and make it come alive within you. The scribes and Pharisees in Jesus' day could quote the Scriptures backwards and forwards, but they were just dead words coming out of their mouths. Christians can do the same, thinking they have power because they remember the right words in the right order. But unless the words you speak are alive, meaningful, and real, just memorizing them will gain you nothing.

In Ephesians, chapter six, you find an important offensive weapon—the Sword of the Spirit—that is God's Word. That does not mean just quoting from the Bible. It means God's Word, quickened by the Holy Spirit living in you, makes a powerful weapon.

> [13] **Therefore, put on every piece of God's armor so you will be able to resist the enemy in the time of evil. Then after the battle you will still be standing firm.**
>
> [14] **Stand your ground, putting on the belt of truth and the body armor of God's righteousness.**
>
> [15] **For shoes, put on the peace that comes from the Good News so that you will be fully prepared.**
>
> [16] **In addition to all of these, hold up the shield of faith to stop the fiery arrows of the devil.**
>
> [17] **Put on salvation as your helmet, and take the sword of the Spirit, which is the word of God.**
>
> **—Ephesians 6:13–17 (NLT)**

When you meditate on the Word, it goes down deep into your soul. When you need it, the Holy Spirit anoints the right passage, which jumps out of your mouth and cuts the enemy like a sharpened sword.

It is a wonderful thing to be able to recall passages of Scripture from memory in order to dwell on them. A friend of mine, Dr. Jack Van Impe, has a nickname: "The Walking

Bible." [3] As a young man he was impressed by a man he knew who could quote Scripture at length. Jack's father, too, practiced memorization techniques and would arrange verses according to Bible doctrine and write them on index cards that he carried with him. It was a means of "hiding" God's Word in his heart whenever he had a spare minute to study them.

Once, when Jack's father went overseas, he left his Bible memory cards behind. Jack found them and started to use them. Soon he found that the verses he "programmed" into his mind were like good friends. They came to his aid when he needed them. Assignments became easier. Witnessing became a natural experience.

Through memorization and meditation, Jack allowed the Word to come alive within his spirit and mind. His successful, worldwide ministry attests to the successes God enabled him to accomplish.

Number Two: To Produce Fruit and Be Effective

In the parable of the sower, Jesus taught that only a quarter of the people who heard the Word would become effective and produce fruit (Matthew 13). Why? What was the difference between rocky soil, shallow soil, thorny soil, and good soil?

One of the major determiners of success was those who *heard* the Word and *kept* the Word would produce fruit thirty, sixty, and a hundred times more.

The Word of God was designed to multiply. Many of us could accomplish thirty, sixty, or a hundred times more than we are accomplishing now if we remembered God's Word. Satan tries to snatch the Word that is sown, and not just the

---

[3] Jack Van Impe website, *Scripture Memorization, The Walking Bible,* http://www.jvim.com/scripturememorization.htm.

Word that brings salvation but also the Word that brings success, prosperity, innovative ideas, creativity, and spiritual maturity. Sadly, he was successful in seventy-five percent of the people in Jesus' parable. Keeping the Word and remembering it causes it to grow. That is how God's promises work.

Number Three: To Remember People's Names

Names are important to people. They are not simply symbolic but carry with them a sense of honor, dignity, and worth. Jesus said the good shepherd knows his sheep by name.

> **"I am the good shepherd; I know my own sheep, and they know me...."**
>
> —**John 10:14 (NLT)**

> **"My sheep listen to my voice; I know them, and they follow me."**
>
> —**John 10:27 (NLT)**

We all want to be known by name. I do not like it when somebody whistles to get my attention or calls, "Hey you!" But when someone uses my name, I feel like they are honoring me.

I learned this when I visited a little Greek restaurant. I walked in and the waitress asked, "What is your name?" I replied, "Dave," and she immediately started addressing me by my name. "Dave, on the menu you will find today's specials." She brought out my beverage and said, "Here you go, Dave." The owner came over and she introduced me to him. He said, "Hi, Dave. Thanks for coming in today." I left a good tip that day because she knew my name and made me feel important and honored.

I enjoyed the experience so much, I went back to the restaurant a week or so later. It was not a fancy place, but the way I was treated there made me feel special. When I came in the same waitress was there. She walked up to me and said, "Hi, Dave. I've got a table right over here for you." I was amazed that she remembered my name when she must meet many people each week. It made me feel like I was important and belonged, and I wanted to take other people there just so I could walk in and have somebody say, "Hi, Dave."

If you are a salesperson or a professional person and you begin to remember people's names, your business will increase. People will trust you, and you will endear yourself to them.

Number Four: To Experience Blessings and Benefits

In Psalm 103:2, God commands us to forget not all his benefits. The word "forget" in the Hebrew language means to mislay. When you forget his benefits, it is as if you set them down somewhere and forgot about them.

A blessing differs from a benefit. God promises blessings, but a benefit is for those who remember them. It is an extra thing given to you by God's mercy.

Some people in the Bible were turned over to the enemy because they forgot God's benefits, like those in 1 Samuel:

> **But the people soon forgot about the LORD their God, so he handed them over to Sisera, the commander of Hazor's army, and also to the Philistines and to the king of Moab, who fought against them.**
>
> **—1 Samuel 12:9 (NLT)**

Psalm 78 says the children of Israel limited the miracles of God because they forgot his wondrous works. Today, many Christians live beneath God's best wishes for them because they forget God's benefits.

MAKING MEMORY WORK

How do you improve your memory? Here are some simple steps.

Number One: Accept the Privilege of Sharing the Mind of Christ

Paul wrote one of the most amazing statements in the Bible.

> [12] What we have received is not the spirit of the world, but the Spirit who is from God, so that we may understand what God has freely given us.
>
> [13] This is what we speak, not in words taught us by human wisdom but in words taught by the Spirit, explaining spiritual realities with Spirit-taught words.
>
> [16] for, "Who has known the mind of the Lord so as to instruct him?" But *we have the mind of Christ.*
>
> —1 Corinthians 2:12–13, 16 (NIV, italics added)

This precept never ceases to amaze me. We can actually share the mind of Christ!

Christ's mind surpasses all the wisdom on this earth. It sees into the deep things of God. Jesus left a last will and testament called The New Testament. Before a will and testament can come into effect, its author must die, and then a living person administers the will. When Jesus died on the cross, he did something that no one else has ever done; He rose from the dead and thereby became the administrator of his own will and testament.

Part of that will is that we share in the mind of Christ. It is part of the inheritance he gives all believers. However, as is true with any inheritance, you must claim your portion of it. You have to accept your privilege under the new covenant to possess the mind of Christ.

93

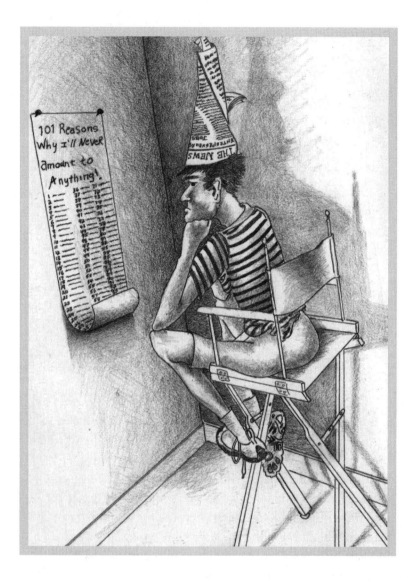

You would never think of allowing a family of skunks to live
behind the couch in your living room. But sometimes
people allow "skunks" to live in their minds.

Believe it! You can share in the mind of Christ! His mind is perfect and all-powerful. It is like hooking up your little "computer" to his universe-sized mainframe and borrowing its power. The first step to having a great memory is having the faith to believe that Jesus wants to share his mind with you.

Number Two: Develop Pure Thinking Habits

Impure thoughts are like skunks you allow to roam in your mind. If you have ever run over a skunk you know how difficult it is to get rid of the smell. You can even take your car through the car wash and it won't do any good.

You would never think of allowing a family of skunks to live behind the couch in your living room. But sometimes people allow "skunks" to live in their minds.

In Philippians, Paul wrote about developing pure thinking habits.

> **Finally, brethren, whatsoever things are true, whatsoever things are honest, whatsoever things are just, whatsoever things are pure, whatsoever things are lovely, whatsoever things are of good report; if there be any virtue, and if there be any praise, think on these things.**
>
> **—Philippians 4:8**

This obviously means you should avoid sinful thoughts like lust and greed and dishonesty, but it also means thoughts that dampen your faith like, "I'm getting old; I can't remember like I used to; I must be getting senile." Careless thoughts are skunks. If you speak badly about your mind, your mind will believe you, and soon you'll have dozens of skunks running around your mind and stinking up your potential!

Pure thinking habits allow God's truth to flow freely. God wants you to have a perfect memory. God wants you to remember his benefits. God wants you to remember whatever you need to remember. Those are the truths you should have running around in your mind!

Number Three: Do Not Clutter Your Mind With Unnecessary Details

Albert Einstein did not know how many feet were in a mile. Why? He did not want to clutter his mind with information he did not need to use. He knew where to look up that fact if he needed to know.

Overload hinders the memory. When I am running a lot of applications on my computer, the memory gets used up and it takes a long time for files to open and commands to process. To make the computer work faster, I have to go through and close a few things I'm not immediately using so there is more memory available to run what I am using.

You can do the same thing with your mind. It takes mental discipline, but you can focus your thoughts. You don't ponder everything that occurs, but decide—with purpose—what will be the focus of your thoughts. Streamline your memory and let go of excess information.

Number Four: Concentrate on What You are Trying to Remember

How many times have you met someone and three minutes later you can't remember what his or her name is? Sometimes you go into a stunned silence and don't give yourself time to retrieve the information.

When that happens, relax and focus on what you want to recall. The memory works better when you are in a relaxed state. Give your mind a moment to retrieve the information. Whatever you do, don't go into a rant about how you're losing your memory. Instead of saying, "I can't remember it right now," say, "Hold on, I can remember this." Give your mind a chance to do its job, and it will become increasingly reliable.

Number Five: Speak Aloud and Repeat What You Desire to Remember

In the Bible, you read about the importance of repetition and remembering. St. Paul, in 1 Timothy and 2 Timothy, told Timothy he would be a good minister if he caused people to remember. The Greek word implies rehearsing and exercising the mind like a physical muscle.

When you meet someone new, repeat his or her name once or twice while you look at his or her face. If there is a fact or figure you want to remember, speak it out loud a few times. Your mind will hear your voice and mark it as something important to remember.

Number Six: Sing and Pray About What You Want to Remember

Many of the Psalms recorded in the Bible are called "songs to bring remembrance." Songs are incredibly effective in helping you to remember. Think of the alphabet song or any other ditty you heard as a child that helped you to remember information.

The Hebrews remembered Scripture by setting it to a melody. Many of the songs sung in churches around the world are taken directly from Scripture. If there is a passage you want to remember, you might try putting it in a song. Who knows, you may be a talented songwriter!

Number Seven: Trust the Holy Spirit to do His Job

One of the tasks of the Holy Spirit on earth is to help us remember.

> But the Advocate, the Holy Spirit, whom the Father
> will send in my name, will teach you all things and
> *will remind* you of everything I have said to you.
>
> —John 14:26 (NIV, italics added)

> Whenever you are arrested and brought to trial,
> do not worry beforehand about what to say. Just *say*
> *whatever is given you at the time*, for it is not you
> speaking, but the Holy Spirit.
>
> —Mark 13:11 (NIV, italics added)

Satan's goal is to steal the Word. The Holy Spirit's goal is to quicken the Word within you and make it powerful against the devil.

You have amazing potential in your memory, and I encourage you to use it to its utmost. You will be more effective in every area of your life. Your marriage will improve as you remember the little things your spouse appreciates. Your finances will improve. You will be more valuable to your boss. You will be more effective at proclaiming the Gospel. You will be more confident in everything you do.

Used together, meditation and memory will supercharge your life!

When you follow the principles discussed in this book, you will become like a tree, planted by the water, bearing luscious fruit!
You will share in the spectacular mind of Christ!

CHAPTER 12

THE LAST WORD

I pray you have found the principles discussed in this book helpful, and you now have a new and better way of thinking about your spectacular mind. Remember:

- Victory and failure both start in your mind
- Wrong thinking can sabotage your success
- Wrong friends can sabotage your success
- Right input leads to right conclusions, actions, and success
- Renewing and renovating your mind is the key to spiritual maturity and success in every area of your life
- Meditating on God's Word transforms your mind from the inside out
- A good memory is one of your mind's most important functions in helping you to achieve success

If you think some are destined for success and others are not—you will always be in the category of those who are not.

The thoughts of the diligent tend only to plenteousness....

—Proverbs 21:5 a

[23] **...Let the Spirit renew your *thoughts and attitudes*.**
[24] **Put on your new nature, *created to be like God*— truly righteous and holy.**

—Ephesians 4:23–24 (NLT, italics added)

You now see how interested God is in helping you to use your mind's full potential and how often the Bible speaks about your mind and how to care for it. It is perhaps the most important tool God has given you. I have faith that your walk with God will improve by developing your spectacular mind and accepting the privilege of sharing the mind of Christ. With him, there is no limit on what you can do!

> *Dear Father,*
>
> *Thank you for the amazing gift of your salvation. Your love for me is perfect, and I thank you for creating me with awesome powers and abilities. I thank you for the treasure of my mind. Please help me to feed my mind with good food, renew my mind with daily study of your Word, and protect my mind from any unclean or negative influences. Help me to share more and more each day in the power and perfection of Christ's mind.*
>
> *—Amen*

About Dave Williams, D. Min.

Dr. Dave Williams is pastor of Mount Hope Church and International Outreach Ministries with headquarters in Lansing, Michigan. He has pastored there for 30 years, leading the church from 226 members to over 4,000 today.

The ministry campus comprises 60 acres in Delta Township, Michigan, and includes a worship center, Bible Training Institute, children's center, youth and young adult facilities, Prayer Chapel, Global Prayer Center, Fitness Center, care facilities, and a medical complex.

Construction of Gilead Healing Center was completed in 2003. This multi-million dollar edifice includes medical facilities, nutritional education, and fitness training. Its most important mission is to equip believers to minister to the sick as Jesus and his disciples did. Medical and osteopathic doctors, doctors of chiropractic and naturopathy, and licensed physical and massage therapists all work harmoniously with trained prayer partners to bring about miraculous healing for sick people from all over the United States.

Under Dave's leadership, 43 daughter and branch churches have been successfully planted in the United States, the

Philippines, Africa and Asia. Including all branch churches, Mount Hope Churches claim over 60,000 members.

Dave is founder and president of Mount Hope Bible Training Institute, a fully accredited, church-based leadership institute for training ministers, church planters, and lay people to perform the work of the ministry. Dave also established the Dave Williams' School for Church Planters, located in St. Pete Beach, Florida.

He has authored 63 books including fifteen times best seller, *The New Life . . . The Start of Something Wonderful* (with over 2 million books sold in eight languages). More recently, he wrote *The World Beyond: The Mysteries of Heaven and How to Get There* (over 100,000 copies sold). His *Miracle Results of Fasting* (Harrison House Publishers) was an Amazon.com five-star top seller for two years in a row.

Dave's articles and reviews have appeared in national magazines such as *Advance, Pentecostal Evangel, Charisma, Ministries Today, Lansing Magazine, Detroit Free Press, World News,* and others.

Dave has appeared on television in the United States and Canada, and has been heard worldwide over "The Hour of Decision," the weekly radio ministry of the Billy Graham Evangelistic Association. Dave's Sunday messages are available for download at www.mounthopechurch.org.

Along with his wife, Mary Jo, Dave established The Dave and Mary Jo Williams Charitable Mission (Strategic Global Mission), a non-profit ministry providing scholarships to pioneer pastors and ministry students, as well as grants to inner-city children's ministries.

As a private pilot, Dave flies for fun. He and Mary Jo have two grown children and one grandson.

CONTACT INFORMATION

Dave Williams' Ministries
P.O. Box 80825
Lansing, Michigan 48908-0825

For a complete list of Dave Williams' life-changing
books, CDs and videos call:

Phone: 517-321-2780
800-888-7284
TDD: 517-321-8200

Or go to his web site:
www.davewilliams.com

For prayer requests, call the
Mount Hope Global Prayer Center
24-hour prayer line at:
517-327-PRAY
(517-327-7729)

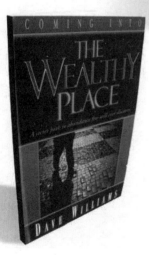